LEADERS IN MY COMMUNITY

I WANT TO BE GOVERNOR

by Jennifer Boothroyd

Consultant: Beth Gambro
Reading Specialist, Yorkville, Illinois

BEARPORT PUBLISHING

Minneapolis, Minnesota

Teaching Tips

Before Reading

- Look at the cover of the book. Discuss the picture and the title.
- Ask readers to brainstorm a list of what they already know about governors. What can they expect to see in the book?
- Go on a picture walk, looking through the pictures to discuss vocabulary and make predictions about the text.

During Reading

- Read for purpose. Encourage readers to think about the state they live in as they are reading.
- Ask readers to look for the details of the book. What are they learning about the job of a governor?
- If readers encounter an unknown word, ask them to look at the sounds in the word. Then, ask them to look at the rest of the page. Are there any clues to help them understand?

After Reading

- Encourage readers to pick a buddy and reread the book together.
- Ask readers to name two things a governor does. Find the pages that tell about these things.
- Ask readers to write or draw something they learned about being governor.

Credits:
Cover and title page, © annebaek/iStock, © Nagel Photography/Shutterstock; 3, © Sheila Fitzgerald/Shutterstock; 5, © zdravinjo/Adobe Stock and © Maksym Yemelyanov/Adobe Stock; 6–7, © adamkaz/iStock; 8–9, © Sean Pavone/iStock; 10–11, © AzmanL/iStock; 12–13, © UPI / Alamy Stock Photo/Alamy; 14–15, © AC NewsPhoto / Alamy Stock Photo/Alamy; 17, © lev radin/Shutterstock; 18–19, © Rob Hainer/Shutterstock; 21, © monkeybusinessimages/iStock; 22T, © wundervisuals/iStock; 22M, © fstop123/iStock; 22B, © SDI Productions/iStock; 23TL, © Ritu Manoj Jethani/Shutterstock; 23TM, © Rob Marmion/Shutterstock; 23TR, © RiverNorthPhotography/iStock; 23BL, © Dave Weaver/Shutterstock; 23BM, © negoworks/Adobe Stock; 23BL, © SeventyFour/iStock.

STATEMENT ON USAGE OF GENERATIVE ARTIFICIAL INTELLIGENCE
Bearport Publishing remains committed to publishing high-quality nonfiction books. Therefore, we restrict the use of generative AI to ensure accuracy of all text and visual components pertaining to a book's subject. See BearportPublishing.com for details.

Library of Congress Cataloging-in-Publication Data

Names: Boothroyd, Jennifer, 1972- author.
Title: I want to be governor / By Jennifer Boothroyd ; Consultant: Beth Gambro, Reading Specialist, Yorkville, Illinois.
Description: Bearcub books. | Minneapolis, Minnesota : Bearport Publishing Company, [2024] |
  Series: Leaders in my community | Includes bibliographical references and index.
Identifiers: LCCN 2023028240 (print) | LCCN 2023028241 (ebook) | ISBN
  9798889162698 (library binding) | ISBN 9798889162742 (paperback) | ISBN
  9798889162780 (ebook)
Subjects: LCSH: Governors--United States--Juvenile literature. | State governments--United States--Juvenile literature.
Classification: LCC JK2447 .B66 2024 (print) | LCC JK2447 (ebook) | DDC
  352.23/2130973--dc23/eng/20230630
LC record available at https://lccn.loc.gov/2023028240
LC ebook record available at https://lccn.loc.gov/2023028241

Copyright © 2024 Bearport Publishing Company. All rights reserved. No part of this publication may be reproduced in whole or in part, stored in any retrieval system, or transmitted in any form or by any means, electronic, mechanical, photocopying, recording, or otherwise, without written permission from the publisher.

For more information, write to Bearport Publishing, 5357 Penn Avenue South, Minneapolis, MN 55419.

Contents

I Want to Lead 4

Be a Leader Now 22

Glossary 23

Index 24

Read More 24

Learn More Online 24

About the Author 24

I Want to Lead

My **state** has many people.

The governor is our leader.

I want to be governor someday!

A governor works hard for everyone in their state.

The people who live there pick the person for the job.

They **vote** for who they want.

Every state has a **capitol** building.

This is where the governor works.

Other state leaders work here, too.

It is a busy place.

Many people work with the governor.

The governor listens to their ideas.

This team helps to solve problems.

Governors have a lot to do.

They help plan how to use money in a state.

This pays for things such as schools and **health care**.

The governor is also in charge of the state's **National Guard**.

This group is part of the army.

It helps people after big storms.

15

States have **laws** for people to follow.

Governors make sure new laws keep people safe.

These laws make the state better for everyone.

A governor tries to keep the land clean, too.

They work hard to make the state a nice place.

The governor wants everyone to enjoy their state.

Being a governor is a lot of work.

Governors need to listen well and make choices carefully.

But I think I could do it!

Be a Leader Now

There are many ways you can be a leader before you become governor.

Learn about the plants and animals that live in your state.

Do what you can to help others after a storm. Send food or water to people who need it.

Listen to your friends. Offer to help them when they need a hand.

Glossary

capitol a building where state leaders work

health care things done that help people be healthy

laws rules that people must follow

National Guard a military group in each state that helps the people there

state an area of land with its own rules that is part of a country

vote to make a choice about someone or something

Index

capitol 9
clean 18
health care 12
laws 16
listen 10, 20, 22
National Guard 15
vote 7

Read More

Chang, Kirsten. *Governor (Our Government).* Minneapolis: Bellwether Media, 2021.

Gaston, Stephanie. *Governor (The Job of a Civic Leader).* Coral Springs, FL: Seahorse Publishing, 2023.

Learn More Online

1. Go to **www.factsurfer.com** or scan the QR code below.
2. Enter **"To Be Governor"** into the search box.
3. Click on the cover of this book to see a list of websites.

About the Author

Jenny Boothroyd hasn't met any governors yet. She has trouble memorizing all 50 state capitals, but she has visited many of them across the country.